POP HITS *for the* INSTRUMENTAL SOLOIST

CD INCLUDED

Play-Along Tracks with Full Performance Recordings!

TITLE

BREAKAWAY

Words and Music by
MATTHEW GERRARD, BRIDGET BENENATE
and AVRIL LAVIGNE

C(9)
Em
D/F♯
C(9)
Em
D/F♯
G
C(9)
Em
D
C(9)
1.
2.
Em
D

A
C
D
cresc.
Chorus:
32
G
D
mf
mf
Em
C
G
D6

Em
D
C(9)
G
D
Em
C
G
D6
To Coda

Em
D
C(9)
decresc.
cresc.
Bridge:
64
D
G2
C6/9
mf
mf
D
G2
C6/9
D
G2
C6/9

D.S. 𝄋 al Coda
Asus
C(9)
D
Coda
Em
D
C(9)
Em
D
C(9)
Em
D
C(9)
p
decresc.
p

WHEN YOU TELL ME THAT YOU LOVE ME

Words and Music by
ALBERT HAMMOND and JOHN BETTIS

Esus
E
Am
Am/G
F(9)
Gsus G
Verses 2 & 3:
14
C(9)
Am11
F(9)
G
G/F
Esus
E
Am
Am/G
F(9)
E
D/E E7
Chorus:
22
A
E/G♯ F♯m7
E
D
Bm7
mf
mf

E D/E E7 A E/G♯ F♯m7 E D Bm7
E
1.
Asus A G
2.
Asus A
Bridge:
32
F G/F F A G/A A F G/F F G F/G G
Chorus:
36
C G/B Am7 G F Dm7
f
f

G F/A G7/B C G/B Am7 G F Dm7
G Csus C G/B Am7 G
F Dm7 Gsus G Csus Am7
decresc.
F(9) Gsus G Csus C(9)
mp
rit.
mf
mp
rit.

EVERYTHING BURNS

Words and Music by
BEN MOODY

Am(4)
G(9)
Am(4)/E
Fmaj13
Am(4)
G(9)
Am(4)/E
Fmaj13
F
23 Chorus:
E7sus
Am(4)
F
mf
cresc.
mf

Dm7
G
Am(4)
F
Dm7
G
Am
G(9)
Am(9)/E
Fmaj7
(with pedal)
35
Verse 2:
Am(4)
G(9)
Am(4)/E
Fmaj13

Am(4)
G(9)
Am(4)/E
Fmaj13
F
E
45
Chorus:
Am
F
Dm7
G
Am
F

53
Dm7
G
N.C.
Am
f
f
F
Dm7
G
Am
F
Dm7
G
Am
mf
decresc.
mf decresc.
F
Dm7
G
Am7
mp decresc.
p

THE NOTEBOOK
(Main Title)

Written by
AARON ZIGMAN

The Notebook - 3 - 1
IFM0518CD

G(9)
A7/C♯
F♯m7
G
B7(♭9)/D♯
Em
Bm7
C
mf
cresc.
mf
Am7/D
D7(♭9)
17
G
a tempo
Cm6/E♭
G
rit.
mp
rit. e dim.
mp
a tempo
cresc.
G+
Em
Am11
Am
D
mf
mf
Gsus2 sus4
G
C
Am9
Am
D7(♭9)
mp
rit.
decresc.
mp
rit.

28
G
a tempo
p
Cm6/E♭
G
cresc.
C(9)
D7/F♯
G sus2 sus4
B7/F♯
Em11
A7/C♯
mf
decresc.
34
Dsus
D
F♯7/C♯
Bm11
Gm6/B♭
D/A
A7sus(♭9)
mp
D
D+
D sus2 sus4
rit.
rit. e dim.

YOU RAISE ME UP

Words and Music by
ROLF LOVLAND and
BRENDAN GRAHAM

C7sus
F
mp
mp
12
Verse:
Csus/F
F
F/A
B♭(9)
(mp)
(mp)
Csus
C
B♭(9)
F(9)/A
B♭(9)
F/C
C7
F
Chorus:
20
Dm
B♭
mf
mf

F/A
C/E
Dm
B♭
F/A
C
dim.
F
B♭(9)/D
F/C
F/A
B♭(9)
F/C
C7sus
C7
1.
F
8vb
2.
F
B♭/F
F
mf
Chorus:
30
Em
C
G/B
D(9)/F♯
Em
C
f
f

G/D
Dsus
D
G
C
G
C(9)/E
mf
mf
G/D
D7sus
D7
1.
G
B/D♯
2.
Em
C
G/D
mp
mp
D7
C(9)/G
G
rit. e dim.
rit. e dim.
p

THE PRAYER

Italian Lyric by
ALBERTO TESTA and TONY RENIS

Words and Music by
CAROLE BAYER SAGER and DAVID FOSTER

C/D
D
poco rit.
14
Chorus:
Em
a tempo
Em7/A
A7
poco rit.
a tempo
F#7sus
F#7
Bm
G
Bm
F#m
G
D/A A
G/D
D
a tempo
poco rit.
poco rit.
a tempo
cresc.
23
Verse 2:
G
A7sus
A7
D
D/F#
mf
mf

G
Asus
A Em/A A
C/D
D7
cresc.
poco rit.
31
Chorus:
Em
a tempo
Em7/A
A7
F♯7sus
F♯7
f
f a tempo
Bm
G
Bm
F♯m
G
D/A A7
mp
G/D
D
cresc.
40
Bridge:
A/G G
A/G
Dsus
D
mf

A/G G A/G
Dsus D
Gmaj7
Dsus D Bm
a tempo
sim.
molto rit.
molto rit.
a tempo
B♭
Gm
Dsus
D
cresc.
49
Verse 3:
C
Dsus
G
G(9)/B
f
f
C
Dsus
D
F/G
G
dim.

57
Chorus:
Am
Am7/D
D7
D7/C
B7sus
B7
mf
dim.
Em
C
Em
Bm
C
G/D
D7
mp
C/G
G
G/F♯
Em
C
Em
Bm
cresc.
mf
sfz
C
G/D
D7
E♭
F
G
f
molto rit.
p

UNTITLED
(How Can This Happen to Me?)

Words and Music by
SIMPLE PLAN

13
G
A
Bm
D
G
A
Asus
A
cresc.
20
Chorus:
D
Bm
G
A6
mf - f
mf - f
D
Bm
G

To Coda
A6
D
decresc.
Verse 2:
30
Bm
D
mp
mp
Bm
D
A
mf
cresc.
38
G
A
Bm
mf

D
G
A
cresc.
Bm
D
G
decresc.
D.S. 𝄋 al Coda
A
Asus
A
cresc.
𝄌 Coda
G
A5
Bm7
D

G
A5
decresc.
Chorus:
57
D
Bm
G
f
f
A6
D
Bm
G
A6
G(9)

INSIDE YOUR HEAVEN

Words and Music by
ANDREAS CARLSSON, PER NYLEN
and SAVAN KOTECHA

Em7 A Asus A Em7 D/F♯ G(9) Asus A
cresc.
cresc.
17
Chorus:
D G(9) D/F♯ Em7 D/F♯
mf
mf
G(9) Asus A D G(9) D/F♯
cresc.
cresc.
Em7 D/F♯ G(9) Asus A D D/F♯ G(9)
f
decresc.
mf
f
dim.

27
Verse 2:
D G/D D G/D A/C♯
mf
Bm C G Em7 D/F♯ G(9) Asus A
35
Chorus:
D G(9) D/F♯ Em7 D/F♯
G(9) Asus A D G(9) D/F♯ Em7 D/F♯
To Coda
cresc.
f

44
Bridge:
G(9)
Asus
A
D
D/F♯
decresc.
mf
dim.
Em7
G(9)
mp
D.S. 𝄋 al Coda
Bm
D/F♯ Em/G F♯m/A G/B
f
cresc.
𝄌 Coda
D(9)
rit. e dim.

TO WHERE YOU ARE

Words and Music by
RICHARD MARX and
LINDA THOMPSON

13
Fm
Gsus
G
Am
poco rit.
mf
mf
poco rit.
a tempo
F
Dm
Gsus
G
Chorus:
17
D
Em11
D(9)/F♯
G(9)
Em(9)
B/D♯
G/D
A7
F♯m7
Bm11

To Coda ⊕
Em7
Gm6
Gm
D
A7/D G/D
D
A7/D G/D
mp
Verse 2:
27
C
Em
F
mp
C
G7
C
Em
Fm
Gsus
G
35
Am
mf
mf

F
Dm
F
G
Am
F
Dm
Gsus
G
D.S. 𝄋 al Coda
𝄌 Coda
43
D
Bm
Em
mp
mp
G(9)
Slower
D
Am7/D G/D
D
Am7/D G/D
D
rit.
rit.
rit. e dim.
p

WHEN YOU SAY YOU LOVE ME

Music by MARK HAMMOND
Lyrics by ROBIN SCOFFIELD

D
F
G/B
C
F6
F/G
G6
F/G
G9
19
Chorus:
C
C/B
Am7
F
G7
C
C/B
mp
1.
Am7
F
G7
F(9)/A
G/B
C

2.
Am7
F
G7
C
C/B
Am7
F
G7
mf
mf
28
Bridge:
Am
Fmaj7
C
3
G
A♭dim7
Am
Fmaj7
F6
C/G
A♭dim7
Am
F
G
rit.
rit.

Chorus:
38
C G/C C F/C G7 C
a tempo
f
f a tempo
G/A Am7 F G7 C Fmaj7 G7
C Fmaj7 G7 F(9)/A F
poco rit.
poco rit.
C C/B Am7 F G C
a tempo
mp
molto rit.
mp
a tempo
molto rit.
p

BRIDGE OVER TROUBLED WATER

Words and Music by
PAUL SIMON

Slowly and majestically (♩ = 84)

G
C G/B Am7 C/G C7
20
F D7 G C C7/E
1.
F Em Dm C Am7 Dm7 Fm6
cresc.
f
f
C F/C C F/C
mp
mp
2.3.
F F♯dim7 C/G Am7 F E7(♯5)/G♯ Am C C7/G

To Coda 𝄌
(after 3rd ending)
33
F
F♯dim7
C/G
Am7
F
E7
Am
D.S. 𝄋 al Coda
(after 3rd ending)
D9
C/G
F
Fm
C
F/C
F/G
mp
mp
𝄌 Coda
Am
Dm
C/G
G
F
Fm
C
rit.
rit.

BREAKAWAY

DEMO 2 PLAY ALONG 3

Words and Music by
MATTHEW GERRARD, BRIDGET BENENATE
and AVRIL LAVIGNE

To Coda
64
Bridge:
mf
D.S. al Coda
Coda
p

WHEN YOU TELL ME THAT YOU LOVE ME

DEMO 4 PLAY ALONG 5

Words and Music by
ALBERT HAMMOND and JOHN BETTIS

1.
2.
32
Bridge:
36
Chorus:
f
mp
rit.

EVERYTHING BURNS

DEMO 6 PLAY ALONG 7

Words and Music by
BEN MOODY

35
Verse 2:
45
Chorus:
53
f
2
mf

THE NOTEBOOK

(Main Title)

DEMO 8 PLAY ALONG 9

Written by
AARON ZIGMAN

Slowly, with expression (♩ = 69)

YOU RAISE ME UP

DEMO 10 PLAY ALONG 11

Words and Music by
ROLF LOVLAND and
BRENDAN GRAHAM

THE PRAYER

DEMO 12 PLAY ALONG 13

Italian Lyric by
ALBERTO TESTA and TONY RENIS

Words and Music by
CAROLE BAYER SAGER and DAVID FOSTER

Bridge:
40
mf
sim.
a tempo
molto rit.
49
Verse 3:
f
57
Chorus:
mf
mp
mf
sfz
f
mp
molto rit.

UNTITLED

(How Can This Happen to Me?)

Words and Music by
SIMPLE PLAN

30
Verse 2:
mp
mf
38
D.S. 𝄋 al Coda
Coda
6
57
Chorus:
f

INSIDE YOUR HEAVEN

DEMO 16 PLAY ALONG 17

Words and Music by
ANDREAS CARLSSON, PER NYLEN
and SAVAN KOTECHA

27 Verse 2:
35 Chorus:
cresc.
To Coda
decresc.
44 Bridge:
f
mf
mp
D.S. al Coda
3
Coda
rit. e dim.
mf

TO WHERE YOU ARE

DEMO 18 PLAY ALONG 19

Words and Music by
RICHARD MARX and
LINDA THOMPSON

To Coda
27
Verse 2:
mp
35
mf
D.S. al Coda
Coda
44
mp
Slower
rit.

WHEN YOU SAY YOU LOVE ME

DEMO 20 PLAY ALONG 21

Music by MARK HAMMOND
Lyrics by ROBIN SCOFFIELD

28
Bridge:
3
3
rit.
38
Chorus:
a tempo
f
poco rit.
a tempo
mp
molto rit.

BRIDGE OVER TROUBLED WATER

DEMO 22 PLAY ALONG 23

Words and Music by
PAUL SIMON